Learn About A Big Book of Animals

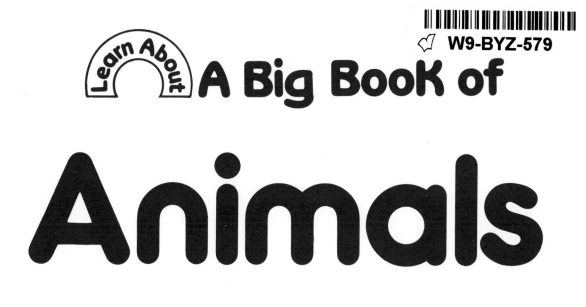

Written by
Bobbie Whitcombe

Brimax Books · Newmarket · England

ARTISTS

Graham Allen
Bob Bampton
Ray Cresswell
Sue Gibson
Bob Hersey
Ian Jackson
Steven Kaye
Alan Male
Aird McKinstrie
Colin Newman
John Rignall
David Thompson
Phil Weare

ISBN 0 86112 505 3
The text and illustrations in this book
have been published as separate volumes.
© Brimax Books Ltd 1988. All rights reserved.
Published by Brimax Books, Newmarket, England, 1988.
Second printing 1989.
Printed in Portugal by Edições ASA—Divisão Gráfica

Contents

Strange Animals

There are many different kinds of animal in the world. Some look very strange to us. Others have some surprising habits.

Look at this strange lizard. The **thorny devil** lives in the deserts of Australia. Its scales are long and spiky. On cold nights, dew forms on them and provides the creature with a drink!

The **giant anteater** has a long snout like a tube. It has no teeth, but it can lick up ants and termites with its long sticky tongue.

The **flamingo** has
a very long neck
and long legs.
It needs a long neck
to reach down into
the water and mud.
It feeds with its head
upside down!

Is this a bird or a mammal? The
duck-billed platypus has a beak and
webbed feet like a duck, but the furry
body of a mammal. It uses its webbed
feet for swimming. But it has claws
to dig its nest. In fact, it is one of
the few mammals that lays eggs.

Animals have some interesting ways of keeping themselves safe from enemies.

The skin of the **armadillo** is covered in scaly, bony plates. They are like a knight's suit of armour, which is how the armadillo got its name.

Opossums pretend to be dead when they are in danger. This one is lying very still until the bobcat goes away.

The **frilled lizard** has a wide fold of skin around its neck. When there is danger, the frill stands up and makes it look fierce. It also opens its mouth wide and hisses to scare its attackers.

The **porcupine** uses its sharp quills as a weapon. If an enemy threatens it, the porcupine charges backwards. It stabs the quills into the animal's face.

The **sea slug** floats on the surface of the water. It feeds on jellyfish. It stores the poison from the jellyfish's long stinging tentacles in its own body. Then the slug can use the poison if it is attacked.

The South American **electric eel** uses electricity to defend itself. It can kill other fish by giving them an electric shock which would be strong enough to knock a man over.

Some animals use their bright skin
colours to warn off enemies.

The **fire salamander**
has bright markings
to warn any predators
that it is poisonous
and dangerous to eat.

The bright colours of
the **arrow-poison frog**
are a warning of
its deadly poison.

The pattern on the
back of this **giant
peacock moth's**
wings looks like a pair
of eyes. Birds think
it is a much bigger
creature than it
really is.

Some animals use disguise to avoid being seen by others.

The **spider crab** has a spiny body which collects weed on it as it moves along. This helps it to hide on the sea shore as it waits to dart out at its prey.

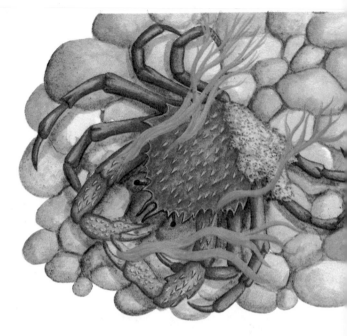

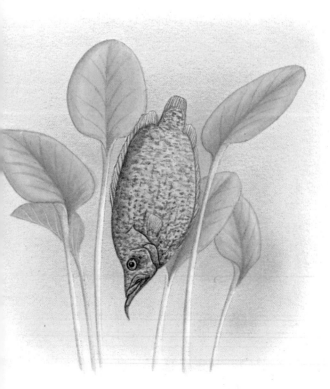

Look at this **leaf fish** standing on its head. It looks like a leaf to any big fish that is passing.

Can you see the
creature on this plant?
It is a **stick insect**.
It moves very slowly
and feeds on the
leaves of plants.
When it is still,
it looks just like
a twig.

The **chameleon** can
change its colour
very quickly so it
will not be seen. Its
tail helps it to hold
on to the branches
and stay still. Then
it shoots out its
long sticky tongue
to catch insects.

There are many strange creatures in the sea. The **dragonfish** protects itself by waving its long fins spiked with poison.

The **copperband butterfly fish** lives in the sunny waters of coral reefs. Enemies cannot tell which eye is the real one.

The **puffer fish** can swallow water and blow itself up into a spiky balloon. Then no creature can manage to eat it!

The **octopus** lives among rocks on the sea bed and catches its food with its eight powerful arms.

The **sting ray** uses its huge fins like wings to help it fly through the water. Can you see the poisonous spine on its tail?

The **angler fish** lives in very deep water. It has a light above its mouth. Smaller fish come close to look and the angler fish gobbles them up.

Why do you think the **pinecone fish** was given that name? It is also known as the pineapple fish.

The silvery fish with lights along its belly is called a **hatchet fish.**

These animals are strange because they can fly even though they have no wings.

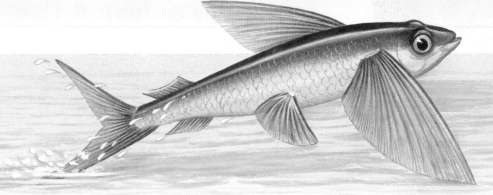

The **flying fish** swims so fast that it shoots out of the water. It uses its fins like wings and flips its tail.
It glides in the air
above the sea.

Adult **salmon** go back to the river where they hatched. They can leap up high waterfalls. At the head of the river where they were born, they lay their eggs and then die.

The **sugar glider**
feeds on the flowers
of trees in Australia.
It has flaps of skin
between its front and
back legs. These act
as a kind of parachute
and help it to glide
from tree to tree.
The female can even
glide with a baby
in her pouch.

Flying frogs have
webs of skin between
their long toes. They
spread these wide and
glide from one tree
to another. They have
sticky pads on their
toes. These help the
frog to hold on when
it lands.

Many animals have surprising eating habits.

Snakes can stretch their jaws open very wide. The African **egg-eating snake** swallows an egg whole. Bones inside its neck crush the shell. The snake spits out the shell and swallows what is inside.

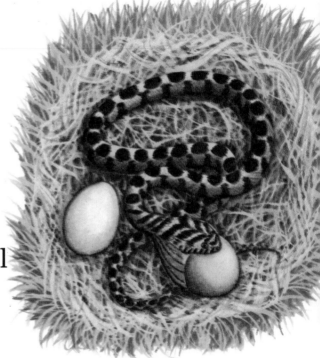

The huge **blue whale** is the largest living animal. It can grow to a length of 30 metres (90 feet) and weigh as much as 30 elephants. But it eats tiny sea creatures called krill. Think how much krill such a large animal must eat.

These animals use tools to help them feed.

The **chimpanzee** pulls the leaves off a small branch to make a stick. It pushes the stick into an ants' nest. Then it pulls it out and eats the ants that cover the stick.

The **sea otter** feeds on fish, crabs and shellfish. It cleverly uses a stone as a tool. It floats on its back and holds a flat stone on its chest. It bangs shells on it until it has cracked them open. Then the otter can eat the soft flesh inside.

Some animals make their homes in strange ways.

Bats hang by their feet with their wings folded up. In the daytime, and in winter, they hide in dark places like caves and attics. These are **horseshoe bats**. Can you see the shape of their noses?

The **water spider** lives in the water but needs air. It carries small bubbles on its hairy body and builds a big bubble under water held in a web. Then it lives in the bubble.

The **beaver** cuts down trees to build
its home on the river. It gnaws at
the trunk until the tree falls down.
Then it gnaws the tree into small logs.

The beaver's home is called a lodge.
It is made of logs, sticks and mud.
It has a hole in the roof to let in air.

The beaver also builds
a dam across the river.
This forms a lake
where the beaver stores
branches as its
food for the winter.

Some animals use others to help them in strange ways.

Look where the
elf owl is perched.
A woodpecker made the
hole in the cactus.
Then the elf owl moved
in with his mate to
make a nest.

The female European
cuckoo lays her eggs
in another bird's nest.
When the owner returns,
it sits on all the
eggs until they hatch.
The young cuckoo is
often bigger than
the other birds and
pushes them out of the
nest. The owner goes
on feeding it until
it is fully grown.

The **remora** has a suction pad on its head.
This sticks firmly to a big shark.
Remoras feed on scraps of food left over
by the shark, and they help to keep its
skin clean. They also get a free ride!

The Egyptian **Nile crocodile** has its mouth
wide open to keep cool. The **plovers** are
picking scraps of meat from between
the crocodile's teeth.

Do you recognise these creatures?
What is strange about them?
There is a list of names at the bottom
of the page to help you.

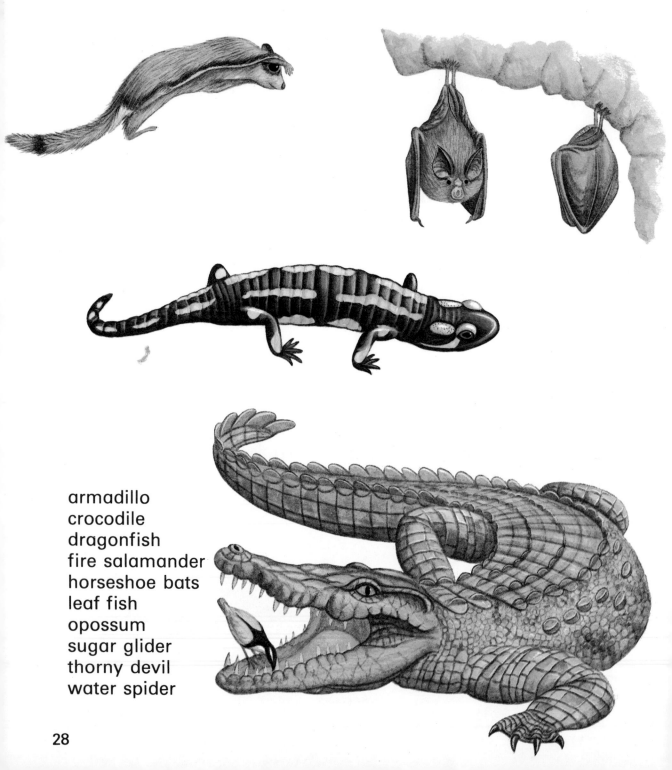

armadillo
crocodile
dragonfish
fire salamander
horseshoe bats
leaf fish
opossum
sugar glider
thorny devil
water spider

Whales and Sharks

The whale family includes the biggest animals that have ever lived. The largest ones are the **blue whales**. They are bigger than any dinosaurs. Whales live in the sea and the water holds up their enormous weight.

Whales are not fishes. They are mammals. They cannot breathe under water and they are warm-blooded. This means the blood in their bodies stays at a constant temperature.

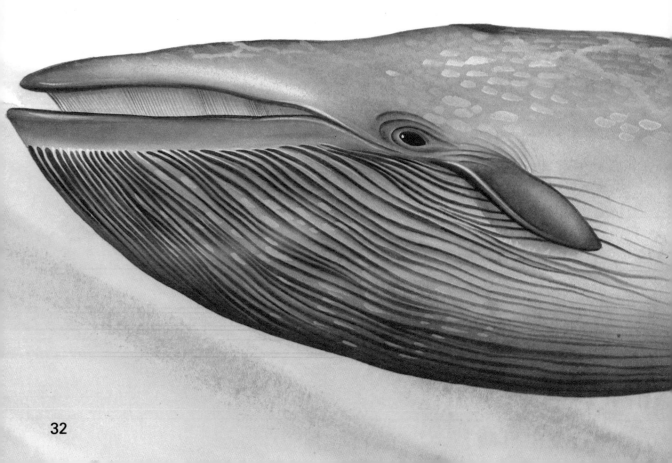

Dolphins and **porpoises** also belong to the whale family. They like to play in the water. These dolphins are following a ship.

Like us, whales use their lungs to breathe.
They have to come up to the surface
and blow out the air from their lungs.
This is called spouting.
Then they take in fresh
air and dive again.

This is a **sperm whale**
It is diving deep to
catch squid. It can stay under water
for a long time.

Some of the biggest whales have no teeth. They have a piece of horn in their mouths called baleen. They feed on tiny sea creatures called krill.

This **humpback whale** swims near the surface of the sea where there is plenty of krill. The whale opens its mouth wide and takes a huge gulp of water. Then it pushes out the water through the baleen, leaving the food behind.

The **blue whale** is the biggest living
animal. It can weigh as much as 30
elephants. But its food is mainly krill.
It eats about 2,000 kg (4,400 pounds)
of krill each day.
The picture shows
what krill looks like
close up. They are
like shrimps. Each one
is about 5 cm (2 inches)
long.

krill

Some whales do have teeth.
They feed on squid and
fish. The **narwhal** is a
white whale with two teeth.
In the males, one of the
teeth grows into a long
tusk.

The **beluga** is also
a white whale but
it has over 32 teeth.
It lives in seas near
the North Pole.

Whale babies grow for about a year inside their mother. A whale has only one baby at a time. A baby whale is called a calf.

This **right whale** calf can drink its mother's milk under water. The calf stays close by its mother for about a year.

This baby **blue whale** has been born
under the water. Its mother pushes it
up to the surface as soon as it is born
so it can breathe. Another female will
swim nearby watching out for danger.

The **killer whale** has sharp teeth. It eats fish, squid, penguins and even seals.
It can swim very fast. Sometimes killer whales leap right out of the water to swim faster.

Look at this **porpoise** leaping out of the water. Porpoises chase and dive for fish in coastal waters.

Dolphins are very clever. They can learn to do tricks like this. They sense things in the water by making high-pitched sounds. The echoes are bounced back by fish or other objects. This helps the dolphins find their prey.

Whales have thick layers of fat to keep
the warmth in their bodies. This is called
blubber. People have hunted whales for
over a thousand years. They used blubber
for oil to make candles and soap. They
also used the baleen to stiffen ladies' corsets.

There are not many whales left now. They are still hunted today for meat and blubber. Some countries have laws to stop people killing whales. It is very sad that man is the worst enemy of these huge, gentle creatures.

Unlike whales, sharks
are fish, not mammals.
They breathe through
flaps behind the head
called gills. Some
sharks are as big
as a boat.

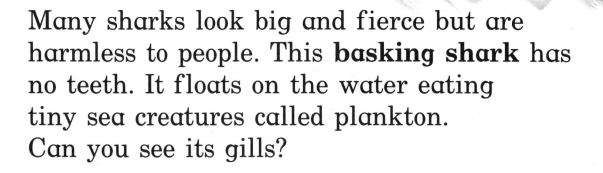

Many sharks look big and fierce but are
harmless to people. This **basking shark** has
no teeth. It floats on the water eating
tiny sea creatures called plankton.
Can you see its gills?

This **whale shark** is the largest fish in the world. It can be longer than a sailing ship. It also feeds on plankton and small fish.

The **dwarf shark** is the smallest of the sharks. It is no bigger than the mackerel shown above it.

This shark is dangerous!
It is the **great white shark**. It eats seals, fish and dolphins. It will also attack people. Look at its sharp teeth.

The **hammerhead shark** is a vicious hunter and may also attack people. It has an eye at each end of its hammer-shaped head.

Look at the **wobbegong** hiding on the sea bed. It pounces out on fish that pass and feeds on them. It is also called a carpet shark. It is dangerous because it is hard to see among the rocks and weed. A swimmer might get a nasty bite on the foot. Wobbegongs live near the coast of Australia.

Like other fish, some sharks lay eggs. Others give birth to live babies. The **hammerhead** has about 30 babies at once. The babies grow inside their mother for about two years. As soon as they are born, the baby sharks swim off in search of food. Unlike whales, they do not need to stay with their mother.

All sharks are very fast swimmers. They
have long slim bodies and strong tail fins.
This helps them to move quickly through
the water. Sharks have a good sense of
smell. They can smell blood in the water
up to half a kilometre away. They will swim
swiftly towards it in the hope of food.
Sharks can be fast and fierce hunters.

Can you remember the names of these whales and sharks?

great white shark
blue whale

hammerhead shark
sperm whale

narwhal
dolphin

killer whale
carpet shark

Animals in Danger

Many kinds of animal are in danger. If the numbers of any kind of animal get very low it may become extinct. This means there will be none left to have babies so the animal will never be seen again.

People are often to blame for this. They may damage the places where animals live. They hunt and kill some animals. Some farmers shoot **brown bears** to keep them away from their farm animals.

Sometimes people kill animals so they can sell their skins or fur or other parts of their bodies. **Rhinos** are hunted for their horns. Some people think the horn can be made into a medicine.

There are less than 1,000 **giant pandas** left in the world. Pandas live in the bamboo forests of China and eat the young shoots. In years when the bamboo does not grow well, there is not enough for the pandas to eat.

For many years people have hunted the big cats for sport and for their skins.

The **snow leopard** lives in the high mountains of Asia. The colour of its coat helps it hide among the rocks and snow. Hunters kill the snow leopard for its beautiful, thick fur.

Jaguars live in the forests and mountains of central and South America. In some places, the trees are being cut down to clear space for farming. This means there is less land for the wild animals to live and hunt in.

56

Tigers live in the jungles of India and forests in Asia. They are the largest of the big cats. For many years hunters have killed tigers for sport.

By the year 2000 some of the handsome big cats may have died out. It is sad to think that this is mainly because of people's greed and the trade in fur coats and rugs.

Many monkeys and apes are in danger.
The jungles where they live and find food
are being cleared for building on.

Golden lion tamarins
are tiny monkeys.
Their homes are
being destroyed. They
are also in danger
from people who
collect them and
sell them as pets.

Gorillas are the
largest of the apes.
As the jungles in
Africa are being
cleared, these gentle
animals are losing their homes.

The **orang-utan** is a large red-haired ape.
It lives most of its life in the trees
but its trees are being chopped down.

Indris look like
monkeys but they
are lemurs. They
live on the island
of Madagascar. They
are in great danger
of dying out completely.

Years ago, there were many **wolves**. But people killed them for their fur and to keep them from harming farm animals. Now wolves only live in wild, mountainous places, far from people.

People have tamed horses for their own use for thousands of years. There are only a few herds of wild horses left in the world. They are **Mongolian wild horses.**

The **rock wallaby** and **koala** are Australian animals in danger. There are not many of these animals because they struggle to find enough food to survive. At one time they were hunted for their skins but now there are laws to protect them.

ring-tailed rock wallaby   koala and baby

The **giant otter**
lives on fish in
South American rivers.
It is hunted for
its fur.

Manatees live
along the American
coast in rivers and
the sea. They are
killed for meat.

Monk seals are now very rare. Fishermen
kill them because they eat fish. Others
die because their water has become
polluted. Some seal
babies do not survive
because people disturb
their breeding places.

This is
a **blue whale.**
Look how big
it is! For many
years people have
killed whales for
their meat and their
fat, called blubber.
Now there are only
a few hundred blue
whales left. Some
countries have laws
to stop whaling.

These are some
reptiles in danger
of dying out.

The **gavial** crocodile is found in India.
It catches fish with its long narrow
snout and sharp teeth. People hunt it for
its skin. They take its eggs for food.

Turtles spend most
of their lives in
water. They are
killed for their meat
and shells. Their
eggs are eaten too.

The **tuatara** lived on earth at the time of the dinosaurs. There are few left because they have been hunted for food.

This is a Fijian **banded iguana.** The forests where these animals live are being cleared. Now there are only a few left.

The San Francisco **garter snake** lives in damp, marshy places. Many of the marshes have been drained to build towns and farms.

Many birds of prey are in danger because they are hunted for sport. People have also destroyed the places where they live.

Look at these large birds. They are **California condors**. Many have been shot by hunters. Now there are only a few pairs left.

The **monkey-eating** eagle is only found in the Philippine islands. The forests where it lives are being destroyed.

Many animals die from swallowing chemicals. Farmers use poisons to kill pests. Factories wash harmful chemicals into seas and rivers. Small animals swallow the poisons. Larger animals eat the small animals and so they too are poisoned. Birds like the **bald eagle** and the **osprey** are in danger because the fish they eat have poison in them.

bald eagle   osprey

Whooping cranes are very rare American birds. They are in danger from hunters. People also drain and dig up the marshes where the cranes live.

The **kakapo** and **takahe** are New Zealand birds that cannot fly. They were safe until stoats, cats and dogs were brought there and killed many of them. Deer also eat the plants the birds feed on.

These **birds of paradise** are hunted for their beautiful feathers. The males spread out their feathers in a special dance to attract the females.

red plumed bird of paradise

king bird of paradise

The **red iiwi** lives in Hawaii. It feeds on nectar from flowers. People used to hunt it to make a cloak for their chief from its feathers.

The **Queen Alexandra's birdwing** is the largest butterfly in the world. It is as big as this page. There are very few left and it is only found in one part of New Guinea.

This big grasshopper is the **giant weta** of New Zealand. It is becoming extinct because it is eaten by rats.

The huge **coconut crab** lives on islands in the Pacific Ocean. It can climb a palm tree and eat the coconuts. People kill it for food.

triton

giant clam

Some shellfish are in danger because people take them for their shells or for food. The **giant clam** shell can be a metre (3 feet) across. Its meat is eaten by people. The shell of the **triton** can be used as a trumpet and is sold to tourists.

The **great raft spider** is nearly as big as your hand. It likes marshy land. Many marshes are drained by farmers. There is now only one marsh in England where it lives.

In this book you have read about many animals in danger. Here are some more. Can you work out why these animals are dying out?

ocelot

woolly spider monkey

everglade kite

alligator

wild yak

kagu

humpback
whale

73

Dinosaurs

About 220 million years ago, the first dinosaurs lived on the Earth. The world was very different. Lands that are now separated by oceans were joined together then. In some places there were swamps. In others there were forests of huge trees. The weather was much warmer. There were no people.

brachiosaurus (brack-ee-oh-sawrus)

Dinosaur means 'terrible lizard'. Dinosaurs were reptiles, as lizards and crocodiles are today. Some of them were the biggest animals that have ever lived on land. The largest were the **brachiosaurus**. Each one probably weighed about the same as 16 elephants. Their nostrils were on top of their high-domed heads.

Most of the largest dinosaurs were gentle plant-eaters. They needed to eat a huge amount and had enormous stomachs. Some swallowed stones to help digest their food! They often lived in herds, like these **apatosaurus.** This protected them from attack by the fiercer meat-eating dinosaurs.

apatosaurus (*ap-at-oh-sawrus*)

Diplodocus was the longest dinosaur. It stretched about 27 metres (89 feet) from head to tail. Look how its long neck helped it to eat the leaves from the tops of the trees.

diplodocus (*dip-lod-oh-cus*)

Some of the dinosaurs did not eat plants.
These were the meat-eaters. They had sharp
claws and teeth. They preyed on lizards,
large insects and other dinosaurs.

tyrannosaurus rex (*ty-ran-oh-sawrus rex*)

Tyrannosaurus Rex was the largest and fiercest of the meat-eating dinosaurs. It stood 6 metres (20 feet) high and moved on its back legs. It only had two fingers on each of its short arms. Each of its sharp teeth was as long as a pencil.

ankylosaurus (*an-kyle-oh-sawrus*)

The big plant-eaters moved slowly and could not easily get away from their enemies. Some of them, like the **ankylosaurus**, were protected by an armour of bony plates. Look at the hard knobby club at the end of its tail. It could swing this hard at any attackers.

Stegosaurus could grow up to 9 metres (29 feet) long. It too had a dangerous tail. Those sharp spikes would keep most enemies away. It also had two rows of bony plates along its back. These may have been for defence. They would also have helped the creature to take in heat if it turned sideways to the sun.

stegosaurus (*steg-oh-sawrus*)

triceratops (*try-sair-oh-tops*)

Some dinosaurs had a frill of bone around their heads and horns on their faces. They had strong mouths like beaks and flat teeth for chewing the toughest of plants. The biggest of these was the **triceratops**, which had three horns. These protected it from its enemies.

Styracosaurus was another horned dinosaur. Its name means 'spiky lizard'. It was 6 metres (20 feet) long and it weighed about 4,000 kg (8,800 pounds). The horn on its nose was 70 centimetres (over 2 feet) long.

styracosaurus (*sty-rak-oh-sawrus*)

If attacked, these dinosaurs would point their horns forward and charge with all the force of their enormous weight behind them.

pachycephalosaurus (*packy-sefa-loh-sawrus*)

Pachycephalosaurus means 'thick-headed lizard'. The heads of these dinosaurs had a dome of solid bone 25 centimetres (10 inches) thick. They probably fought each other with their heads to decide who was to be leader of the herd.

Look at the long bony crest which **parasaurolophus** had on the back of its head. Its jaws looked like a duck's beak. Inside its mouth were hundreds of small sharp teeth. It used them to eat leaves. When it stood up, it was as tall as a giraffe.

parasaurolophus (*para-sor-ol-oh-fus*)

At the same time as the dinosaurs, giant reptiles swam in the seas. **Plesiosaurs** were up to 13 metres (42 feet) long. They ate mainly fish. With their powerful flippers, they could swim backwards as well as forwards. **Ichthyosaur** means 'fish lizard'. Ichthyosaurs were good swimmers. They ate fish and shellfish, which they crushed with their long snouts and sharp teeth.

plesiosaurs (*pless-e-oh-saws*)

ichthyosaurs (*ik-thee-oh-saws*)

pterosaurs (*ter-oh-saws*)

There were flying
reptiles in the air
too. They were called
pterosaurs. They had
a sheet of leathery skin
between their long arms and
their back legs. The smallest
were only as big as a blackbird.
The largest had a wing span
of up to 12 metres (39 feet).
This is four times as wide as
the biggest bird today.

There are no dinosaurs alive today, but their bones can still be found. When some of these creatures died their bodies fell into muddy rivers or the sea. Over many years, the mud or sand built up and hardened into rock. The bones then became fossils. Some fossils are found when the rock splits or if it is worn away by rain and wind.

Sometimes people find fossils when they dig in mines or quarries. The bones are carefully cleaned and fitted together to show people what the creature looked like. You can see dinosaur skeletons in museums.

The age of the rocks in which fossils are found tells us how long ago the creatures lived. Fossil records show that the dinosaurs disappeared from the earth about 65 million years ago. The giant flying and swimming reptiles died out, too. Why did this happen at that time?

Probably it is because over thousands of years the earth had become colder. The dinosaurs could not eat enough to keep their bodies warm and had no fur or feathers to keep the heat in. When the plant-eaters died out, the meat-eaters grew short of food. So the dinosaurs became extinct.

Now you have read about many different dinosaurs. Can you recognise these ones?

apatosaurus
plesiosaur
stegosaurus
ankylosaurus
diplodocus
triceratops

parasaurolophus
pterosaur
pachycephalosaurus
styracosaurus
ichthyosaur
tyrannosaurus rex

Animals of the Night

When we are asleep at night, many creatures are awake. These are called nocturnal animals. They hunt for food in the dark and rest during the day.

Most moths fly at night. They can smell the scent of flowers that open at dusk. This **privet hawk moth** uses its long tongue to drink nectar from the honeysuckle.

The tiny **mouse deer** feeds on leaves in the forests of Africa and Asia. It is about the size of a dog and very shy. It feels safer at night when most of its enemies are sleeping.

Wood mice come out at night. They feed on seeds and berries. But there are other animals about, hunting at night for their prey. Look out, mouse! The owl is coming.

Weasels are nocturnal hunters. The weasel can move very fast, and catches mice and rabbits. But it must beware of owls and foxes too.

Many night creatures hunt on their own.

The African **web-throwing spider** hides during the day. At night, it spins a stretchy web. When an insect comes along, the spider throws the web over its prey, then eats it.

The **moonrat** likes to stay away from other animals. It gives off a nasty smell and snarls to keep away attackers. Moonrats feed on insects and worms.

The **linsang** lives in the forests of Asia. It is good at climbing and pouncing. It hunts alone for birds, small animals and frogs during the night.

Some other animals hunt at night, but in large groups. African **hunting dogs** have long legs and can keep on running till they tire their prey out. The pack can chase antelope or zebra for many miles across the plains.

Hunting in the dark is not easy. Many creatures of the night have sharp senses to help them.

Look what big eyes the **tarsier** has! It can see well even on very dark nights. It has good hearing too, and can turn its ears towards the faintest sound. When a tarsier rests, it keeps one eye open.

The **leopard gecko** is a kind of lizard. It has large round eyes which see very well in the dark. Geckos can climb steep rocks and even run upside down to catch insects at night.

This **raccoon** is fishing. It uses its paws to feel the water move. This means a fish is coming. Then the raccoon flips it out and eats it.

Moles live mainly under ground. Their eyes are small and weak but their hearing is good. They use their whiskers to feel any movements in the soil. This warns them of danger.

Other night creatures use their ears to
help them find food and to avoid danger.

The **aye-aye** taps on a branch and listens.
It can hear where the wood is hollow.
It nibbles at the wood and uses its long
middle finger to scoop out insects
to feed on.

Foxes have a keen
sense of hearing.
They can move their
ears backwards and
forwards. This helps
them to hear any small
animals moving about
at night.

Bats have small eyes and weak eyesight.
They sense shapes and movement by sending
out very high-pitched squeaks. The echoes
are bounced back by objects around them.
They can sense thin branches and even
telegraph wires so they do not bump
into things at night. This special sense
also helps them find moths and other
insects to feed on.

Some night creatures have a strong sense of smell.

The **polecat** uses its sense of smell to help it hunt for mice, rabbits, birds' eggs and frogs in the woods at night.
It also marks its home with its own scent. Other polecats can smell it and keep away.

The South American **armadillo** can smell its food even under the ground! When it smells insects or other small creatures, it digs very fast. It holds its breath while it is digging.

Some snakes have a special sense which helps them to hunt in the dark. They are called pit vipers. This **rattlesnake** is a pit viper. There is a pit on either side of its head near the eye. This can sense changes in heat caused by another animal approaching. The snake glides silently towards the animal and injects it with poison. This **kangaroo rat** is in great danger.

Nocturnal creatures often need to move quietly as they hunt for food.

Night birds have soft edges and tips to their wing feathers. They make no sound as they fly. As this **barn owl** swoops down, its prey does not hear it coming.

Bird-eating spiders can dart out at their prey without making a sound. Sometimes they catch small birds, but mainly they eat insects and lizards.

The **genet** is like
a cat in the way it
follows its prey.
It crouches low
and then pounces.
It can move quietly
on softly padded feet.

The **loris** eats insects
and sometimes small
birds. It can cling
on to branches and
keep very still for
a long time. It creeps
up silently to its
prey and then grabs it.

Many nocturnal animals have dark colours. This helps them to avoid being seen.

Look how the dark coat of the **black panther** helps it to hunt at night. It catches monkeys, birds and other animals in the jungles of Asia.

The New Zealand **kiwi** scratches on the ground for insects and berries. Its dull colour makes it hard to see in the evening light.

Creatures of the night do not have
darkness to hide them when they sleep
during the day. They have to use other
ways of hiding.

The **frogmouth bird**
keeps very still.
Its colour helps it
to hide in the tree.
The **moth** is hiding
too. Can you see it?

Wombats hide in burrows under ground.
They can dig tunnels half a mile long.
The wombat comes out at night to eat
grass, bark and roots.

Some creatures live where it is always night because there is no light.

Olms live in pools in caves where it is always dark. They are nearly blind.

There is no light at the bottom of the ocean. Some deep-sea fish give off light from their bodies, like these **hatchet fish** and **viper fish**. This helps them to see one another in the dark.

hatchet fish

viper fish

At the North and South poles, it is dark all day in winter.

These **penguins** live on the ice in the Antarctic. It is very cold there. A thick layer of fat helps them to keep warm.

During the long Arctic winter the **polar bear** is also a creature of the night. There is less food about then, but polar bears travel hundreds of miles over the ice hunting for seals and fish.

kingfisher

Arctic tern

pintail duck

Canada geese

Many birds travel to other countries for part of the year to find better feeding grounds. This is called migration. These birds all migrate. Some migrate at night. They use the stars to guide them. They come down to the land to rest and feed in the day time. The birds in the sky are **Arctic terns**. They fly over 13,000 kms (8,000 miles) to spend the winter in Antarctica.

In the daytime we can easily watch animals. It is not so easy at night. The darkness makes it hard for us to learn about nocturnal creatures. Now we can use a special light to see animals in the dark. An infra-red light is shone on these **badgers** so that people can film them.

Here are some animals of the night.
Can you name them and say what is special
about them?

hunting dogs   raccoon   olm   armadillo

barn owl   hatchet fish   rattlesnake   skunk   bats

Reptiles

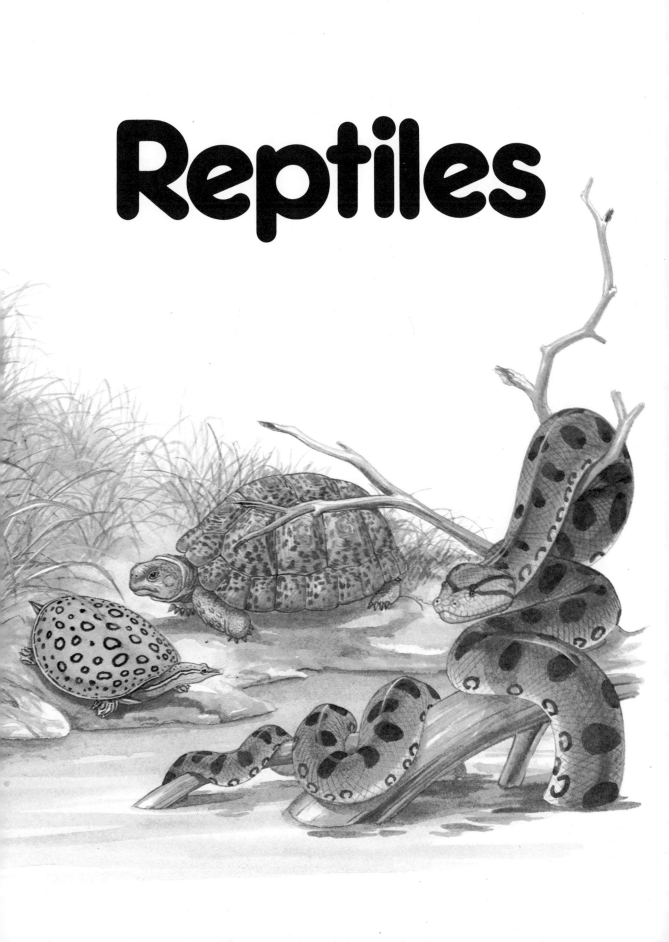

There are over 6,000 different kinds of reptile. Crocodiles, lizards and snakes are reptiles. So are turtles and tortoises.

Reptiles have lived on Earth
for millions of years. They
are found mainly in the warmer
parts of the world. Some live
on land and some live in water.
Some even live in trees. All
reptiles have scaly skin.

Reptiles are cold-blooded.
Their blood does not
keep their bodies
warm. They get heat
and energy by lying
in the sun, like
these **chuckwallahs**.
Their waterproof skin
stops their bodies drying
out. When it gets
too hot, they
find a shady spot.
This **lizard** is cooling
down in the shade of
a leaf.

Reptiles all lay eggs.
Almost as soon as
they hatch out, the
babies are able to
look after themselves.

In countries where it is not hot all year round, snakes, lizards and tortoises may hibernate during the winter.
Can you see the **tortoise** under the leaves? And this **snake**? They hide in warm, dry places until spring.

Crocodiles and alligators are very similar creatures. Alligators are only found in one river in China and in the southern United States. **Crocodiles**, like this one, live in swamps and rivers in many hot countries. With webbed feet and strong tails, they are good swimmers. They can also move surprisingly fast on land!

Alligators and
crocodiles keep warm
in the sun. If it
gets too hot, they
slip back into the
water, or open their
jaws wide. This **alligator** is
letting the air cool it down.
It cannot lose heat by sweating
as we do. At night it goes back
into the river, as the water stays
warmer than the air around.

Young alligators and crocodiles
eat fish, frogs and crabs. As they
grow bigger, they eat larger
animals. This **crocodile**
is lying in the water
with only its eyes and
nose showing. It waits for
an animal to come down to drink.
Then it seizes the victim
in its powerful jaws.

Tortoises, turtles and terrapins all belong to the same group of reptiles. They have a strong hard shell which protects them from their enemies.

Tortoises have high, rounded shells. They move very slowly. They can hide from their enemies by pulling their head, legs and tail inside the shell.

Turtles and terrapins live in water. They are very good swimmers. Look at this **pondslider turtle**'s webbed feet.

Giant tortoises are found on the Galapagos Islands in the Pacific Ocean and a few islands in the Indian Ocean. They eat grass, leaves and berries. They can be over a metre (3 feet) long

Marine turtles live in the sea. Their strong flippers are good for swimming but not for walking. Only the females go ashore, to lay their eggs.
The **leatherback turtle** does not have scales.
It has a shell that is like hard rubber.
The female lays up to 100 eggs in the sand and then returns to the sea.

The female **green turtle** has come ashore to lay her eggs. She digs a hole in the sand and lays about 100 eggs. She covers them with sand. The heat of the sun will help to hatch them. 60 days later the baby turtles will scramble down the beach to the sea.

frilled lizard

flying lizard

plated lizard

wall lizard

blue-tongued skink

green lizard

bearded dragon

gecko

Lizards can be found in all parts of the world. Some live in trees. Some live in deserts. Many of them, like the skinks, are good at burrowing in the sand. The flying lizard of south-east Asia has flaps of skin which help it glide from tree to tree. Lizards feed on insects, small animals and sometimes eggs and fruit.

The smallest lizards are the geckos. The dwarf gecko is only a few centimetres (1½ inches) long. The largest are the **Komodo dragons**, found on some Pacific islands. They can grow to over 3 metres (10 feet) long. They prey on animals as big as a wild boar.

Chameleons are lizards which live in trees. Look how their toes curl round and grip the branches. They move slowly and also use their tails to hold on with. They can change colour if they are angry or scared and to help them to hide.

The chameleon's eyes can look in different directions. When it sees an insect, it shoots out its long, sticky tongue very fast to catch it.

The **marine iguana** is
the only lizard that
spends most of its time
in the sea. It feeds on seaweed. These
creatures live on the Galapagos Islands
near South America. In the day, they bask
on the rocks in the sun. When it is very
hot, they crowd together in shady crevices
or slip into the sea to cool off.

There are nearly three thousand different kinds of **snake**. Many are harmless. Some are able to inject poison through fangs in their mouths into their prey. Others kill their prey by coiling round it and squeezing hard. Snakes test the air with their tongues. They "smell" food this way. They have no teeth. Their jaws can open very wide so they swallow their prey whole.

Indian cobra

coral snake

egg-eating snake

boa constrictor

python

These snakes are not dangerous to people.

This is a **grass snake**. Grass snakes like to live in damp places. They are good swimmers and eat fish, frogs and sometimes birds' eggs.

The **hognose snake** lives in North America. It defends itself by spreading its ribs and doubling in size. It rolls onto its back and pretends to be dead. If pushed the right way up, it will roll over again!

These snakes are dangerous.

Rattlesnakes are
found in America.
Their bite is poisonous.
The rattling sound
made by the tail
is a warning to
keep away!

Cobras can spread the skin of their necks
into a hood when they are alarmed. This
snake rises up and strikes down at its
prey with its fangs loaded with venom.
Cobras are found in warm parts of Africa,
South America and Asia.

These snakes squeeze their prey and stop them breathing. They are members of the boa constrictor family.

The **anaconda** is as long as a bus. It swims in the water of South American rivers, looking for its food.

This is the longest snake in the world. It is the **reticulated python** found in south-east Asia. It can be 9 metres (29 feet) long. After it has killed its prey, it opens its jaws wide and swallows it whole.

Here are some of the reptiles you have read about in this book. Can you recognise them?

alligator   tortoise

      chameleon   cobra

Komodo   dragon   turtle

lizard   crocodile

Dangerous Animals

In this book you can read about dangerous animals and what makes them dangerous.

Some animals are dangerous because they are big and fierce. Tigers are the largest of the big cats. Look at this **tiger**'s sharp teeth. It is hunting for animals such as deer, wild pigs and cattle. An old or injured tiger may attack humans.

Some small creatures can be as dangerous
as larger ones. Look at the way this **scorpion**
holds its tail. The sharp sting stabs
into its prey and poisons it. The poison
from some African scorpions can kill
a person within hours.

The large spider is
a female **black widow
spider**. She is very
dangerous. Her bite
is poisonous and can
sometimes be fatal.
The male is harmless,
though.

The animals here are meat-eaters. They may attack people if they are hungry.

Crocodiles live in hot countries. They lurk in marshes and rivers, waiting to catch animals that come to drink. With most of its body under the water, this crocodile looks like a floating log. Look at its powerful jaws.

Look at the size of this **anaconda**! This South American snake lurks in the water for an animal to come to the water's edge. It kills by wrapping itself around its victim and crushing it.

Lionesses are hard to see in the long, dry grass. They hunt for meat for their families. They will stalk a deer or zebra and then attack swiftly. When they are too old to catch other animals, lions may attack people.

These animals do not attack people for food. But they may be dangerous if they think they are in danger themselves.

Grizzly bears live in the North American forests. They feed mainly on fish, fruit and leaves. When it stands upright, the grizzly is taller than a man. It is very strong. It can kill large animals with one blow of its paw.

The **cassowary** is a bird which cannot fly. It can run fast and has strong legs. It lashes out with these if people get too close. Its powerful kick can kill a person.

Gorillas are the biggest of the apes. They look dangerous but they are gentle. They attack only if someone frightens them. An angry male will beat his chest, roar and may charge at a stranger.

Most animals are dangerous when they are looking after their babies.

This **Cape buffalo** will charge at anyone getting near her calf. She fights fiercely and uses her long horns and sharp hooves. The lioness had better keep well clear of those pointed horns!

The **harpy eagle** is guarding its nest. Look at its feet. Each one is bigger than your hand. It uses its sharp claws and beak to attack anything that comes near its chicks.

The **giant panda** looks like a big cuddly toy, but it can be dangerous. The adult is big and heavy. It has strong paws with sharp claws. A female panda will hit out to protect her young cub. She even keeps the male away.

Many animals become dangerous if they are hurt or frightened.

The **rhinoceros** is a shy creature with poor eyesight. But if it is startled by a noise or sudden movement, it may attack with its long horn. It can run fast and will even charge at cars!

Elephants are gentle animals. They can be trained to help people in their work. Look at these **Indian elephants** moving huge logs. There are some people who shoot elephants for their ivory tusks. A wounded elephant will charge at a hunter.

Some animals are dangerous when there is a large group of them together.

Wolves hunt in packs. They can kill an animal as big as a moose. They attack again and again until the animal is weak. Then they kill it. When they are hungry, wolves may attack people.

Hyenas hunt in packs too. They often attack a wounded animal, like this wildebeest. They can crush the biggest bones with their strong jaws. The vultures will feed on the leftovers.

Look at the sharp teeth of these **piranha** fish. They live in South American rivers. They are small, but a shoal of them can eat a big animal.

Insects can be very harmful to people, especially when there are hundreds of millions of them in a swarm together. **Locusts** travel great distances eating everything growing near them. They destroy all the crops for miles. Then people and animals may starve.

There are some deadly creatures in the sea.

This is a **hammerhead shark**. It has a very
good sense of smell. Can you see its
nostrils, set wide apart on its head?
It waves its head from side to side as it
hunts for its prey. If it smells blood,
it swims fast to attack with its
sharp teeth.

Look at the long tentacles of this **Portuguese man o'war** jellyfish. This creature can give a painful sting to humans.

The Pacific **octopus** has eight arms. Each arm can be up to 5 metres (16 feet) long. Rows of strong suckers on its arms grip its prey, which it kills with a fierce bite. It could be dangerous for a swimmer to be caught by these arms!

Some creatures can be harmful to people because they carry disease.

The **vampire bat** is found in South America. It can pass disease from animals to humans by biting them. Can you see its teeth?

Mosquitoes live near ponds and marshes. Some kinds of mosquito carry diseases like malaria and yellow fever. They pass the disease by biting people.

Rats live all over the world wherever there are stores of food. Look what these black rats have done! Because they sometimes live in dirty places, rats can carry disease. Then the food they have touched makes people ill.

Flies eat rotten food which is full of germs. They can carry the germs to food that humans then eat. The germs can make humans ill.

Some snakes are poisonous. They bite their victim and inject venom into it with sharp fangs.

This African **boomslang** is a tree snake. It lies hidden in the branches and strikes suddenly at its prey. Its venom can kill a person.

The **Indian cobra**'s bite can be fatal too. It rears up like this before striking. As well as biting, some cobras can spit poison at their victim.

There is another very dangerous animal. These creatures hunt and kill many other animals. They are changing the world around us. They cut down forests and spill deadly poisons onto the land and into rivers and lakes. They are very clever. They have invented the deadliest of weapons. This creature has the power to destroy the land and all the animals on it. The most dangerous animal is **man.**

Do you recognise these animals?
The names at the bottom of the page will help.
What makes these animals dangerous?

harpy eagle   Cape buffalo   piranha
tiger   crocodile   vampire bat   Indian cobra

Insects

There are thousands of millions of insects in the world. There are more different kinds of insect than all the other kinds of animal put together.

All insects have six legs, like this **earwig**. Many have wings, like this **butterfly**. Insects do not have bones like us. They have a hard outer skin. Insects breathe through holes in their sides. Can you see the breathing holes on this **praying mantis**?

You may think these creatures are insects but they are not.

Spiders belong to a different family from insects. All spiders have eight legs not six.

Centipedes have many more than six legs. Can you count them all? They also have many parts to their bodies. Insects have only three parts to their bodies.

Look how big the eyes of this **bee** are. Insects' eyes are made up of many small parts. They stick out from the head. The insect can see all around and fly quickly away from danger. Insects can see colours and patterns on flowers that we cannot see.

This close-up picture shows the feathery feelers of a **moth**. Insects have feelers called antennae on their heads. They can smell food and feel movement in the air with these. Some male moths can smell females miles away.

Insects do not have ears. But some insects can hear very well. They use sounds to signal to each other. The **cricket** hears with its legs. Can you see the ear hole near its front knee? The cricket rubs its wings together to make a chirping sound.

The hairs on insects' bodies are often used to taste and feel things. This **fly** has tiny hairs on its feet. These can taste sugar.

Insects eat in many different ways.

Look at the **butterfly**'s long tongue. It is like a tube. The butterfly uses it to suck nectar from flowers.

The **housefly**'s mouth has a pad like a sponge. The fly wets the food, then soaks it up with the pad.

A **cockroach** has very strong jaws. It can cut up and chew plants and small animals. Cockroaches also like to eat any left-over bits of food they can find.

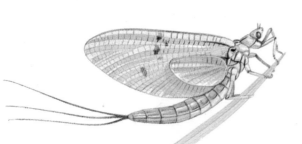

The adult **mayfly** does not eat. It only lives for one day. When it has laid its eggs it dies.

These **honey ants** are used to store honey. They spend all their lives hanging upside down in the nest. When there is no food outside, the rest of the ants feed on honey from the fat honey ants.

Insects go through different stages as they grow from eggs into adults.

The mother **cricket** lays her eggs in the earth.

A baby cricket hatches out of one of the eggs.

When the cricket grows too big for its hard skin, the skin splits and the insect leaves it behind. This is called moulting.

Insects moult up to ten times before they are fully grown.

Butterflies change their shape completely
during their lives.

The female **peacock
butterfly** lays her eggs
on a nettle leaf.

A caterpillar hatches
out of one of the eggs.
As it grows,
it sheds its skin
several times.

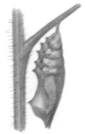

The caterpillar spins
a covering called a
cocoon. Inside this,
its body changes.

A butterfly comes
out of the cocoon.

Look at the different
butterfly eggs.
Each kind of
butterfly lays eggs
of a different shape.
The female butterfly
lays her eggs on
a plant that is
the right food for
her caterpillars.
Then she leaves them.
When the caterpillars
hatch out they eat
the leaves.

Can you see what is
hiding in the bubbles?
A young **froghopper**
has hatched out of
its egg. The froth,
which we call cuckoo
spit, keeps it safe
from birds.

Some insect mothers stay and care for their babies. Look at this **earwig**. She waves her pincers to scare away enemies. She looks after her young and feeds them until they can find their own food.

Army ants are always on the move, searching for food. They take their young with them. The adults carry the young in their mouths.

Insects have many enemies. But some insects are hard to see. This helps to keep them safe.

Which thorn is the real one? The **thorn bug** looks just like a thorn when it keeps still.

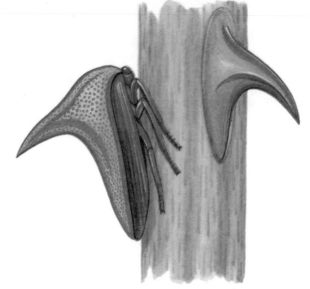

Can you see the **stick insect**? It feeds on the leaves of plants. When enemies are near, it does not move.

This **butterfly** looks like a leaf on the stem of a plant.

Look closely for the **peppered moth**. It is well hidden on the tree bark. It is hard for its enemies to see it.

Some insects have other ways of keeping safe from enemies. This African **grasshopper** is brightly coloured. This warns birds that it tastes nasty. The bird will leave the grasshopper alone.

The **bombardier beetle** can scare off its enemies. It makes a popping noise and shoots out a nasty smelling gas.
This spider is choking on the gas while the beetle gets away.

Wood ants squirt out poison at creatures that try to eat them. The frog keeps out of the way.

Here are some strange insects.

The **Hercules beetle** is
one of the largest
beetles in the world.
It is as large as
a person's hand.

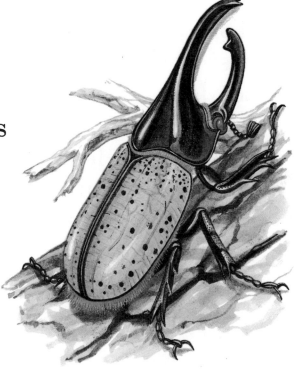

Fireflies and **glow worms** are also beetles.
They can make a light at the end
of their bodies. During the day they hide
away. At night they come out to feed.
They use their lights to find each other
in the dark.

Some insects live together in large groups.

Honey bees make a nest of wax. The queen bee lays her eggs in the cells. The adult bees help to feed the young. They all gather honey and store it in the cells.

Termites make nests out of soil. There are many rooms inside, joined by tunnels. Some nests are as high as a small tree. Millons of termites live inside this nest.

Other insects live alone.
The **mole cricket**
lives undergound. It
digs out tunnels with
its large front legs
and feeds on roots.

The female **potter wasp**
makes a nest like a pot
out of mud and clay.
She fills it with
caterpillars and
lays an egg. When the
young grub hatches
out, it eats the
caterpillars.

Some insects can be harmful.

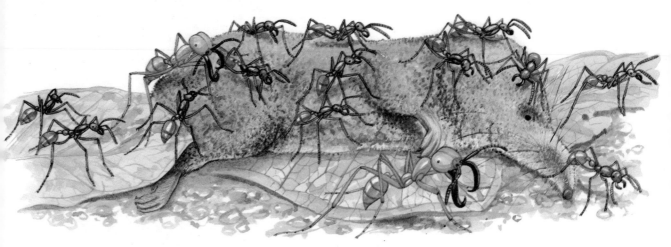

Some eat the crops that we grow, or hurt animals. Look at these **army ants**. In hot countries they march along in big groups. They attack and eat any animal in their path. This shrew did not get away in time.

Mosquitoes can be dangerous. In some countries, they can spread diseases like malaria, which makes people very ill. The mosquito bites people's skin and feeds on their blood.

Some insects are helpful to us.

Bees collect nectar from flowers. They make honey and wax. They carry pollen on the hairs of their bodies from one plant to another. This helps the plants to make seeds and fruit.

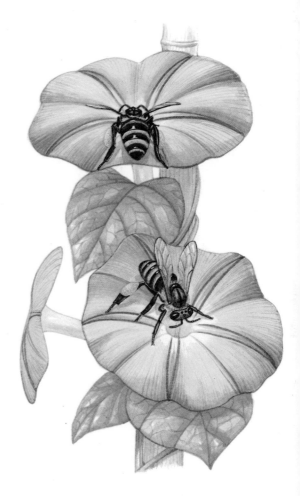

Ladybirds eat small insects called greenfly. This is helpful because the greenfly would damage plants like this rose. Ladybirds are also called ladybugs.

Which of these creatures are insects?
What is special about them?

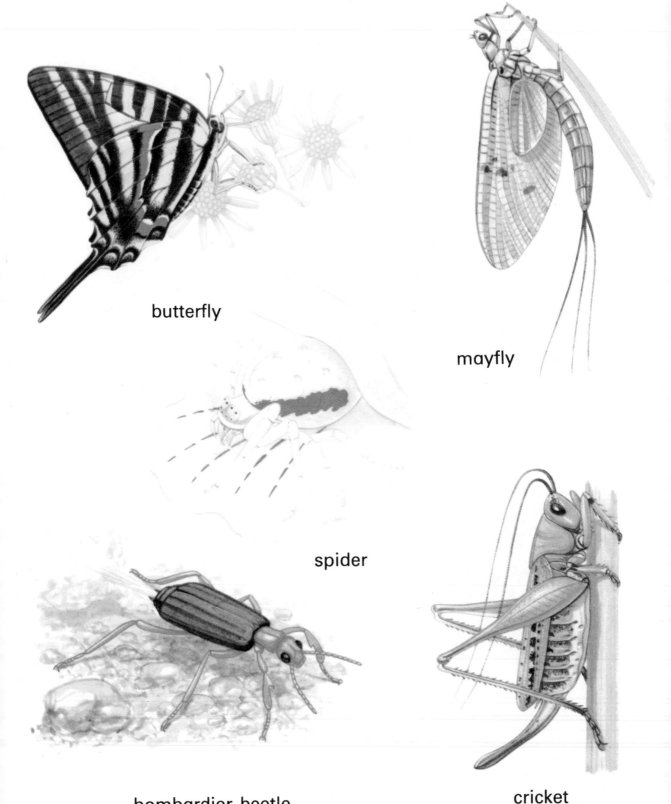

butterfly

mayfly

spider

bombardier beetle

cricket

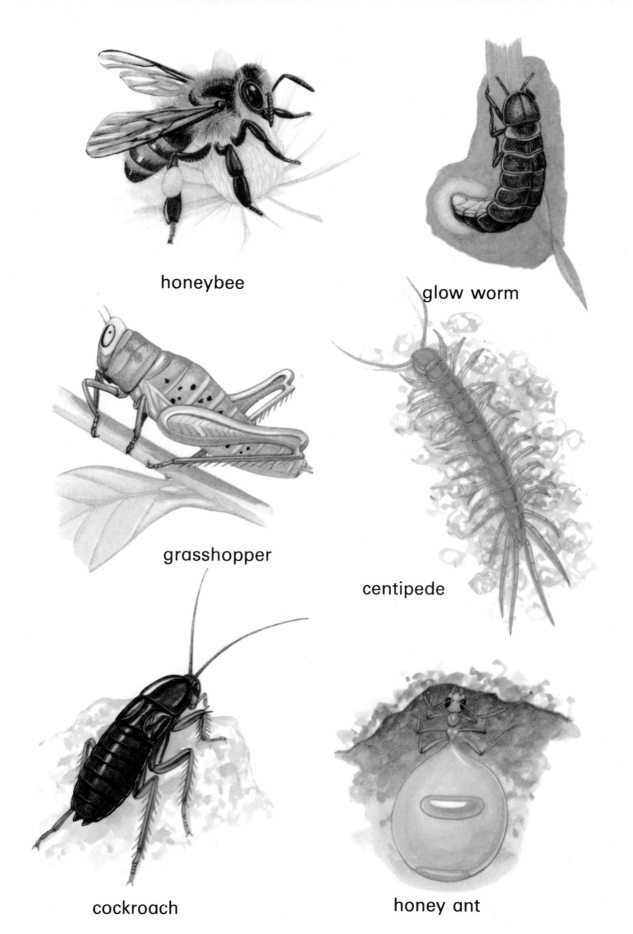

honeybee

glow worm

grasshopper

centipede

cockroach

honey ant

Animal Facts and Fun

Animal Facts

Animals live all over the world. Some live in the most difficult places. Their bodies are suited to the places they live in.

Penguins can live in the icy Antarctic because they have a thick layer of fat under their feathers.

Look at the **musk oxen**'s long shaggy coats! They are well protected against the Arctic winter.

In hot, dry places, animals need to keep cool.

Lizards are well
suited to hot countries.
They do not need much
to drink. Their tough
skins stop their bodies
drying out in the sun.

The **Arabian camel** can survive well in the
desert. It can go without water for six
days. Thick eyelashes protect its eyes from
bright sun and sand. In a sandstorm
it can close its nostrils too.

In the South American rain forest, it is always damp and the trees grow very tall. Many animals are suited to life in the forest.

These **spider monkeys** have long, strong arms and tails. They can climb and swing high in the trees as they gather fruit.

The **tree frog** has extra large tips to its toes. These help it grip on to the leaves and branches.

There is not much to eat on the forest floor. But the **tapir** uses its snout to pull leaves off the bushes. Its flat feet help it to walk on swampy ground.

Many animals live on the grasslands of Africa. The **giraffe** is well suited to finding food which other animals cannot reach. Its long neck means it can eat leaves from acacia trees. Some can be as high as the upstairs window of a house.

Gazelles eat grass. They feed in herds. They stand in open land so that they can see any enemies approaching. They are well adapted to escape because they can run fast.

Many birds are specially suited to feed in a particular way. Look at all these different shapes of beak.

The **hummingbird** sucks nectar from flowers with its long bill. It beats its wings up to 80 times a second to hover in one place.

This **macaw** lives in the Brazilian jungle. It can crack Brazil nuts with its strong beak!

The **crossbill** really does have a crossed bill! It uses it to pick seeds out of pinecones.

Some animals travel long distances to find food or to breed. We call this migration.

In autumn, **swallows** fly all the way from Britain to South Africa and go back the next spring.

Monarch butterflies spend the winter in California and Florida. In spring, they fly 2,400 kms (1,500 miles) north to lay their eggs.

Wildebeest may travel thousands of miles in a year. They can sense rain up to 50 kms (30 miles) away, and move towards the fresh grass.

Some animals build homes for themselves and their families.

A **squirrel**'s nest is called a drey. It is built out of twigs and moss high in a tree.

The female **polar bear** digs out a den in the snow. The cubs are born and live here through the Arctic winter.

Badger families live in underground homes called sets. Some sets are over 50 years old. They keep the set very clean, bringing in fresh leaves for bedding.

Birds are clever at building homes in many different ways and places.

The South American **ovenbird** makes a nest of mud. The sun bakes the mud hard. The way in is curved, so enemies cannot get at the chicks.

The Indian **tailor bird**'s nest is made of two leaves. The bird pushes grass through the leaves to hold them together.

Kittiwakes build nests of seaweed on cliff ledges. Their eggs are pointed so that they roll round, not off, the edge of the cliff.

All animals have babies. Some lay eggs and then leave them to hatch on their own.

The female **cod** can lay 5 million eggs. Only about 5 of these will live to be adult fish.

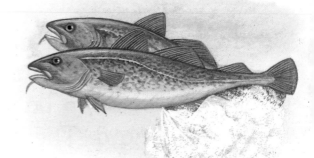

The female **toad** lays thousands of eggs. Most are eaten by fish or birds. Only a few grow into toads.

Some animals look after their eggs and young. Birds keep their eggs warm with their bodies. These **mute swans** take turns sitting on the nest.

The female **wolf spider** carries her eggs in a web underneath her. When the eggs hatch, she carries the babies on her back.

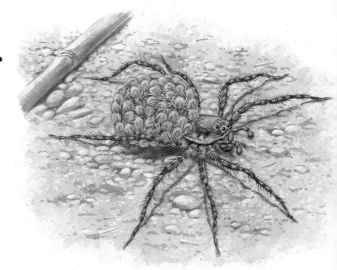

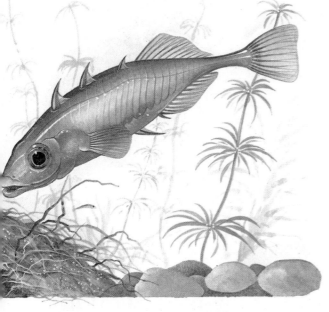

The male **stickleback** makes a nest of weed and sand. Then the female lays her eggs in it. The father guards the eggs and looks after the babies.

When baby **Nile crocodiles** hatch out, the mother carries them to the water in her mouth. She stays with them until they can look after themselves.

Mammals are animals that do not lay eggs. They give birth to live babies and feed them on milk from their bodies.

Virginia opossums have up to to 14 babies at once. They stay in their mother's pouch for 10 weeks. Then they ride on her back, clinging to her fur.

The new-born **wallaby** is tiny and blind. It climbs into its mother's pouch and feeds on her milk. After about eight months it is big enough to get out. But it climbs back in if there is danger.

The female **gibbon** carries her baby everywhere. The baby must hold on tight, as its mother swings through the trees!

The **elephant** calf can follow the herd a few hours after it is born. It feeds from its mother and holds on to her tail when it is tired.

197

Here are some animal record breakers.

The largest insect
in the world is the
African **Goliath beetle**.
It is as big as
a man's hand.

The biggest moth is
the **Hercules moth**
found in Australia.
Its wingspan is
28 cm (11 inches).

The largest living animal is the **blue whale**.
It is bigger than any dinosaur and can
weigh up to 146 tonnes (160 US tons).

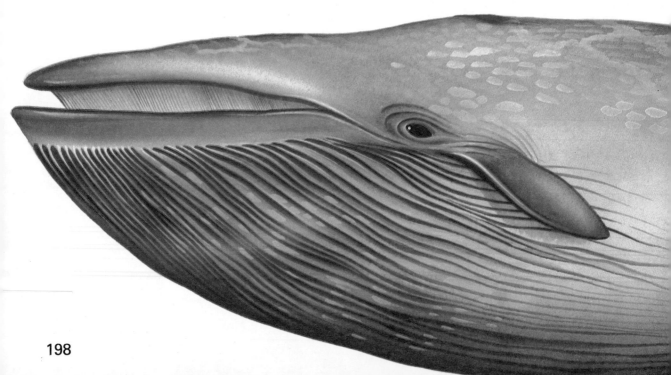

The **giraffe** is the
tallest animal in
the world. It can
grow up to 6 m
(19 feet) high.

The common **flea**
is only the size of
a pinhead, but it can
jump up 18cm (9 inches).
That is 130 times its
own height.

The **bee hummingbird**
is the smallest bird.
It is only 5cm (2 inches).
Its egg is the size
of a pea.

The smallest mammal
is the **pygmy shrew**.
It is about as long
as your little finger.
It feeds on insects as
large as itself.

The fastest flier is the **swift**. The spine-tailed swift can fly at over 170 kph (106 mph).

The fastest swimmer at 109 kph (68 mph) is the **sailfish**. It swims faster than the cheetah runs.

The fastest runner on land is the **cheetah**. It can run at 105 kph (65 mph) over short distances. But some **antelopes** can run at 50–65 kph (30–40 mph) for up to 6 km (4 miles).

Animal Fun

When is a fox not a fox?

. . . when it is a
flying fox. This bat
sucks the juice
from ripe fruit.

When is a cat not a cat?

. . . when it is a polecat.
This member of the
weasel family has
a long, bushy tail.

When is a goose not a goose?

. . . when it is a mongoose. This mammal
can climb trees. It likes to eat birds'
eggs and can even kill a snake.

When is a horse not a horse?

... when it is a seahorse.
This fish swims
upright in the water.

When is a lion not a lion?

... when it is a sea-lion.
It has ears on the
outside of its head
and uses its flippers
to move about on land
and in the water.

When is a worm not a worm?

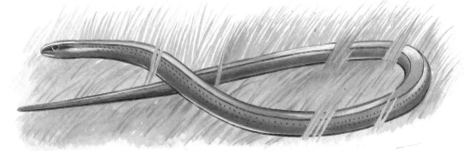

... when it is a slow-worm. This is really
a lizard without any legs. It feeds on
insects and worms.

Here are some of the animals you have read about. Can you recognise them?

badger

Virginia opossum

seahorse

sea-lion

lizard

flying fox

tree frog

cheetah

wolf spider